W... ... Ey...
of the Needle

White Eye
of the Needle

*A collection of poems on
love, life and lockdown*

CHRIS CAMPBELL

THE CHOIR PRESS

First published in the United Kingdom in 2021 by
The Choir Press

ISBN 978-1-78963-181-4

For my beautiful wife Rowa, Mum, Dad, Matt, Maddy, Elliot, and the Tahas.

Praise for *White Eye of the Needle*:

'These poems are sparkling with affection. Campbell finds beauty in the everyday, in the connections to each other and to the land. In a world when we are feeling cut off, these poems are like a bridge back to some sense of balance. They are celebrations of relationships, places and of being alive. Some of them feel like a home I've never been to.' – **David Linklater**

'Stunning, sensual and subtle. In *White Eye of the Needle*, we see a clear love of language with a deft alertness to the power of sound and what it can create. Combined with stunning images, this is a book to give those you love.' – **Katherine Lockton**

'Chris Campbell's poems are accessible, enjoyable, and formally and stylistically thoughtful and dextrous – as in 'Yellow dress', which empathetically slips into and out of ballad metre, or the well-pitched epigram 'Time doesn't slow', or the subtle uses of slant-rhyme and couplets in 'Last night of our honeymoon', in which 'We eat side by side, the candle facing us, / The taps of shoes are circling // But beside us, a restaurant sits empty, / Laid out cutlery and glass'. A lot of the explorations in these poems are personal, but this is no solipsist's diary: he is constantly conscious of the power a poet can have to touch someone's heart by revealing his own.'
 – **Rory Waterman**

'At a time when the world feels a little darker, *White Eye of the Needle* invites the reader to gaze upon a world where "houses rub shoulders", "the taps of shoes are circling" and dawn spreads its welcome light "like the oranges brightening Seville". In this tender, wistful collection, Campbell observes humanity with a sharp eye – where the lockdown poems offer a relatable and searingly honest depiction of our days transfixed on blinking screens, there is always the human touch to offer relief in a lemon dress, the notes of 'Für Elise', tumbling hedgerows and the tender simplicity of a shared meal with a loved one. Like the flowers that push through its city gardens, this is a collection that reminds us that it's the human connection and the power of the natural world that keep hope alive in a world gone dark.'
 – **Natalie Ann Holborow**

'The poems in Campbell's *White Eye of the Needle* serve, like the landform the book is named for, as both frame and portal. As a frame they help contain life's experiences of love and loss and, as a portal, they allow us to look through to the inner heart of what matters. The subtle use of rhyme, control of form and an attention to the things of life – olives, bicycles, clothes – give the collection colours and textures which sit comfortably alongside the white space within the poems, and the illustrations which complement them. This collection is an accomplished capturing of moments.' – **Claire Dyer**

Contents

Yellow dress

You pose in a yellow dress
On a heated patio,

Smile as cool as Tignes:
It resists the midday sun.

I want to pause a minute
As you stroke your curled, dark hair,

For a lockdown seems forever
Without your beauty there.

Olives sunbathe in their oil,
Swelter side by side,

Our hedge slumps over brick,
An aged window pipes out bakhoor.

I sweat, still, burning this to memory,
You glisten like an *Asanga*,

Dress draws me in, a gentle tide,
Curves soft in lemon.

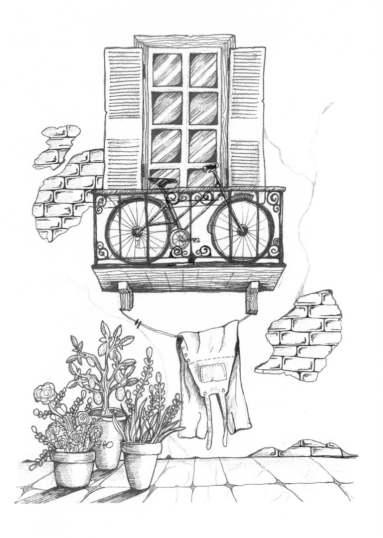

You shine

Sparkling in our holiday nest.
Fan fluttering in your hand, breeze lifting hair

Held back by fingertips. We kiss and rest
Basking in Milan's glittering glare

Then sip our coffee, shrouded in warm shade.
Your mind spreads across the table as you read

Slides for a speech. Outside, children's cries now fade
Like early bird calls, hatchlings before feed.

Dark, battered shutters cling to pink walls,
Bicycles on balconies and potted

Plants by the neighbours' drying overalls.
Reciting scooped up corrections you spotted,

Your yellow and white striped top seems
Sweeter than all of Italy's ice creams.

Mister Painter

Houses rub shoulders,
Paint falls like peeling skin
And I ask where the sea is

Amongst the rubble and the dirt: a small face–
School kids back off the bus. They joke,
Skip and dance, and the hills roll in

The background like silent guardians,
Waiting for the rain.

An old man grips a rubbish bag
Like a painter needs his pots,
'Paint this part, Mister' say the kids,

Pointing at gaps in the houses. And he sweeps
His brush, coarse as a wave, heavy
As rain. This too will age.

Synchronised buskers

Sun shines on the canal and through our window
On *Castle Boulevard*. Joggers and cyclists

Along a normally busy road, but on a Sunday
Morning in cold October air, there are gaps

In traffic, revealing boats like sitting cats in
The *Kitty Café*. A woman walks towards the

Train station, suitcase in hand, past the castle
On the cliff, cocooned in scaffolding, supporting

Visitor trade like *Hooters* on a Saturday.
Even through steel barriers, it's something to admire,

Like other parts of this East Midlands city.
Dainty delis, cocktail bars and independent shops

Scatter through the centre, between the chain
Stores and worn shopping centres that add to the city's weight,

So not to float down the canal. *Paul Smith*,
Closed *Jamie's Italian*, and the elderly

Shoemaker shouting to a crowd. The city hall hums
Prestige, gently synchronising with the buskers

And fruit market sellers; 'Pears for a pound,
Pears for a pound'. The discount shops, the trainer

Stores treading their authority, in a city
Stamped with gyms. The ice hockey stadium that sells

Hotdogs outside on match nights–fans pour into
The centre as floods fill the roads and nearby,

Art galleries, independent theatres and
Nottingham Playhouse showing ballet during Black

History Month. '*Doughnotts*' for the sweet tooth, sports bars
For footy fans unable to make the Forest

Or Notts County games–and a nail bar colours a
Side road. Students educate the streets with hoodies

And ripped jeans, while surgeons, doctors and nurses stay
Up all night on late shifts. Sirens regularly pass,

Ambulances like Ubers–we're in safe hands;
As traffic breaks, sunshine reveals the beauty of the canal.

Cages

We laughed at *Hackney City Farm*
Pointed to animals in sunshine
I held your elbow:
All you'd let me touch
But that felt hopeful
As if our bones connected
Through the thin cotton
Of your white summer dress
Our light hold, almost primal
Laughter released from cages.

Mr Cat

You look at me wide-eyed, Mr Cat
Green pools like holiday brochure oceans

Sit high on top of the sofa
Surveying your world from above

Sharing your play den with our presence
We convert the lounge and bedroom into office space

Paws rest in front, ears twitching at every scrape
As neighbours move out furniture

No one will disrupt your kingdom, Mr Cat
Of toy mice, a scratch post, food bowl and litter tray

Life might change outside these walls, but you grow
Bigger inside. You've already doubled in size

Without the takeaway trays, empty bottles, sunken sofas
And open history browsers with half-searched mini-breaks

You chew plants and think we're not looking
Like a child swiping sundown snacks

As we pull out hair over a *Zoom* or *Teams* meeting
Clinging to coffee, daydreaming about trips abroad

We almost see you thinking; slow blink, a slightly tilted head
You know we don't like it but you paw and bite leaves

Pretend to scour the ceiling, the walls,
Before going back for another crunch

Monitoring spiders then, distracted by your tail,
You pounce on it; a pest entranced by you, the Pied Piper

Where were you in the Madagascan bush when frogs leapt
From toilet seats and a snake tucked its head under our pillow?

Your tail's part of you, growing like your claws that scratch
    the sofa,
Torso that reaches up the chimney, unsettling dust

Your whiskers, your beautiful markings that evolve and
Change like a feline chameleon–but grey, white and beige,
    almost pink

Paws remain soft, your fur shines at four months old
And you purr deeply when touched in the mood

Meows are high and soft, unless it's early morning
And you can't find us

We continue our hunt for a break for fresh scenery
But know your realm is hard to leave; your chest fur white
    like a beach

This is your kingdom, Mr Cat, though you'll never venture
    outside,
Your eyes are deep and bright like a holiday brochure ocean.

Dawn

When exhausted birds have flown away and tweeted their
    last breath
that's when I'll close my eyes and say there's more to life than
    death.

For when they call, they call with heart through feathered
    chest
and as they go, they fly with hope that after song they'll rest.

And I in bed as next day looms and dawn begins to stir,
think back before this sombre place to sunlit gardens far.

A silent bird that sings no more may have no song to make,
but as I lie in deepened thought, my bitten nails, break.

As once it sang, brought the day and closed it with a verse,
now every time I think of it, my anxiety gets worse.

Take my clothes, my pillow too and place me by the tree
where these poor birds once posed and sang and breathed
    relief to me.

Trainers

In fields of yellow daffodils
and grass as fine as hair,
that's where my chest beside you once
grew under torn trainers.

Like cats that toy with life,
we chance, pounce and play,
I count the years, and 'til we stroll again,
all blue skies will feel grey.

Would it comfort you?

Waking up in your old house?
Fresh toast tussling memories of eggs with soldiers,
your aged grey bath lies ready
for you to soak in bubbles after rugby,
smudge marks on the windows where
you wave to the family Springer,
sliding doors out to the garden; Wisteria,
two planted trees that steadily grow
branches like birthdays,
and a bedroom light switch bows in anticipation,
flick on and off to tease your brother–
the walls and ceilings the same
but all the people changed.

Chimney snorkels

We reach a corner and catch a couple
Hand in hand–keep our distance,

Fingers away from our faces.
The light has faded, unveiling

The moon; a crescent with a single star
Below–as if they arrived to a night's party together.

The canal glistens, narrowboats like guards on shift,
Replacing daytime geese patrol.

From thin, black chimney snorkels,
Smoke invades the crisp air, putrid and thick,

A woman sits in a saloon, back to the open door,
Asserting a point to male companions.

The cafés and pubs look empty, but in the
Distance a 'Pizza' neon sign bends the horizon,

Who has the dough for electricity while
No one bakes and not a soul visits?

Underneath a bridge, a man waits by the path,
His coat is zipped up tight; he seems bemused,

Anxious. Flashing an impatient look, his eyes
Brighten in the dark. He lets us pass in silence.

I gesture a thank you–his mouth looks like it opens,
But it hides behind a mask.

Hurdles

Wind speeds across our patio
Dragging the cardboard sheets
Our newly-moved in neighbours sit on;
A substitute for garden furniture
Unable to be bought
Before the lockdown. Now

Sheets lift and fall as if completing
A hurdle race; hard edges hit
The ground like tired competitors
Slumping in heat. The beaming sun is
Social distancing far from us
A crowd of one–watching from on high

Its glare affecting the competition
Like a constant iPhone flash. Still intact,
With a few knocks, cardboard taps the window
As if not wanting to self-isolate either.

Catch light

We soak up rays; the last of evening light in
A small corner of our courtyard garden,

Our restless cat at the window pawing at greenflies.
A flowerpot in sunshine guards the back door

While our well-watered hedge slumps into the neighbour's
Garden like a nuisance guest who's overstayed

His welcome. In the quiet, but for the sound of traffic,
I imagine the hedge shouting profanities at neatly-pruned

Wall climbers who were minding their own business.
The buttons on his drink-stained shirt popped,

Like mini corks, revealing a pale pot belly.
Our flowerpot reaches to the heavens. I envisage her

Rolling her eyes, all high and mighty on top of her clay,
Ordering a taxi to speed up the hedge's exit.

The cat has left the windowsill and preens.
I look for shears.

Newborn's sunshine

A white stork flies ov'r West Wycombe Hill
Delivering a bundle to *Stoke Mandeville*
With the tender newborn
Comes a memorable dawn
Like the oranges brightening Seville.

Must all the world's beauty be a gift?

Your smiles enrich the brightest place,
expensive presents last much less than this,
no jewels can beat those eyes upon your face.
Our plastic wealth of plucked lips; nip and tuck,
takes all attention from our individuality
and tries to rid all life of natural luck,
adding to inner ugliness that never sags.

Careful what you touch

People pass on the pavement with urgency again.
Where once was the odd stroller, now restrictions have eased;

There's ten. A man in a cardigan, woollen
Trousers and a patterned shirt, with a large man bag,

Crosses the street. He's got dark brown boots with thick laces
Strapped to his feet. He passes a couple, both in

Pale shorts and oversized sunglasses and picks up
The pace. At the bus stop another man, in suit

And tie, sticks out his arm, mask covering his face.
An elderly fella kneels by a shop window,

Trousers torn, tapping his phone. Shop's closed, if it wasn't
Would he still be alone? Security guard–

Hands on hip, mask on face, minds a queue. If there's
No toilet roll in this supermarket can

I sell some tissue? A woman dressed in black,
Hair tied back, rubs gel on her hands. Another

Mask floats past–be careful what you touch. In lockdown,
People-watching is like fare dodging: no

Ticket's bought. But the outcome hurts
Now you're coughing up; caught.

Virtual coo

The first time we see him or her
I bet it's over *WhatsApp*.
His or her smile, their gurgle,
Their cry of confusion at the world.
Or, perhaps, needing burping or winding or Mum.
I'll see the glint in Dad's eyes over WiFi,
His proud grin, the little one in his arms.
We'll make silly noises over our mobile screen
And hope the signal is strong enough
As we snap our delight, send admiration,
Make plans to see them in the not-too-distant
Future, from two metres. But now we celebrate
In our own way, giving a virtual hug and coo.

Man upstairs

The man upstairs won't answer my call;
His thunderous noise all day is awful.
Turn down the TV's roar,
Switch it off and open the door–
I pray for a hush that's eternal!

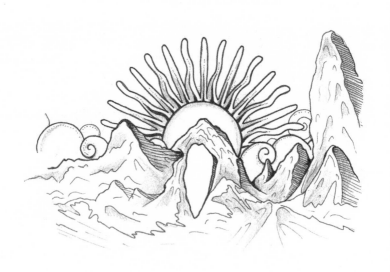

White eye of the needle

We crouch inside the snow-capped
Eye of the needle

Pose for a photo,
While fingers fumble in gloves

The view frames us in ice
Next to a steep black run

Helmets hold goggles,
Cold as found treasure

We almost kiss as boots
Crunch in the snow

White glistens near
Like jewels under sun

I see a sparkle in your eyes,
Buried behind dark lenses

We stand, hurried as hares,
Our skis and poles a climb away.

Hit the slopes

You   hit
the   slop
-es,   one
ski   bes-
ide   ano-
ther,   head
tow-   ards
the   next
run   and
pray   you'
-re   no-
  t   n
   o   w
    c   o
    l   o
     ur
      b
      l
      i
      i
      i
      i
      n
      d
      .

Illustration

Mild hunger is
an open book
full of blank pages.
You snack
on the page numbers;
gradually become fuller,
until you find
a chapter–
each one a different course.
The cover,
your placemat,
bookmark like cutlery,
an illustration to savour
like dessert.

St Ives café

Where scones, jam and cream,
sit proudly on the counter above
today's catch: sea bream.
The waitress in her overalls–all
white but with a stain,
where chocolate cake and lemon
slice slipped after serving mains.
And beside the café's tables,
where tourists escape the rain,
is the art of local residents
to show why they remain.

No holding me back

Your soft lips are the gateway
to a weapon so sharp,

for your tongue is an adder
striking poison through my heart.

Let down the drawbridge,
clear out the moat,

I'll battle on, whether by
foot, horse, or boat.

No arrows will harm me,
no spears hold me back,

my Achilles: your voice
confirms our love's no longer intact.

Tomatoes ripen

Tomatoes ripen sweet in sun,
Red roses grow against wind,
Nets of fresh fish caught for market.

No line cast down into the sea
Could hook memories of you,
Your quiet jokes and joyous smile.

Our thoughts stay above surface,
Of your flat caps and smiling eyes,
Nets of fresh fish caught for market.

We think on your advice and those
Happy life reflections you shared,
Your quiet jokes and joyous smile.

Jumping in yours and Grandma's bed
When little–you heading for work,
Nets of fresh fish caught for market.

Toasted cheese sandwich for breakfast,
Later, Sinatra on CD,
Your quiet jokes and joyous smile,
Nets of fresh fish caught for market.

Time doesn't slow

Time doesn't slow down to save me,
So why should I speed up to save time?

Last night of our honeymoon

You glance across the table, lift a glass
As the bar fills up beside us

A French couple arm in arm, then another,
Laces cut into bare feet

Middle-aged partners, singletons, drink
In one hand, experience in the other–

The chatter thickens like smoke
We squeeze further into our corner,

Now half-sat on a piano stool
I move my chair again, my legs pressed

Tighter under the table, almost touching pedals
I imagine the notes of *Für Elise*,

As bar hum beats into our conversation
Zebu and fresh fish arrive

We eat side by side, the candle facing us,
The taps of shoes are circling

But beside us, a restaurant sits empty,
Laid out cutlery and glass–

Waiting as I did under the arch:
Last night of our honeymoon.

Biography

Chris Campbell, born in Dublin, is a former national and regional journalist who worked for newspaper titles in London, Bristol, Bath, South Wales and Gloucestershire. Chris has a passion for poetry, writing and travel and has judged young writer competitions in Swansea. He graduated with an MA in Journalism from Kingston University and a BA (Hons) in Economic and Political Development from the University of Exeter, with a year's study in Uppsala, Sweden. He currently lives in Nottingham.

Sandra Evans is a graphic designer and illustrator with over 20 years' experience in the media industry. Growing up in South Wales, she began drawing from a very early age and took inspiration from all the nature around her. She has a degree in Illustration and worked as a creative designer at the South Wales Evening Post newspaper. Based in Swansea Bay, Sandra now works as a freelance graphic designer and artist. She is passionate about wildlife and the environment and lives a vegan lifestyle.